J 629.28 Broekel, Ray
BR
         I can be an auto
         mechanic

$13.27

DATE			
JC 9 '91	JL 27 98	AG 09 '08	
OC 29 '91	OCT 06 99	NO 27 08	
MR 12 '92	DEC 14 99		
OC 1 '92	AG 30 99	JP 16 10	
MAR 19 '94	JA 13 00	DE 02 10	
AUG 13 00	JY 05 01	JY 26 10	
NOV 29 97	JY 09 '01		
APR 20 98	JY 12 '02		
JUN 25 98	AG 05 02		
JUL 10 98	JY 14 03		
	NO 23 05		

I CAN BE AN AUTO MECHANIC

By Ray Broekel

Prepared under the direction of Robert Hillerich, Ph.D.

For Gus, Harold, Tom, Eddie, Lonnie, and all the others to whom I take my car when it needs fixing. They work with their hands and heads just as I do.

CHILDRENS PRESS ®

CHICAGO

Library of Congress Cataloging in Publication Data
Broekel, Ray.
  I can be an automobile mechanic.

  Includes index.
  Summary: Explains what an auto mechanic does,
discusses important qualities such as manual dexterity
and an ability to work with computers and math, and
examines the special education and training required for
such a career.
  1. Automobiles—Maintenance and repair—Vocational
guidance—Juvenile literature. [1. Automobile mechanics.
2. Automobiles—Maintenance and repair—Vocational
guidance. 3. Occupations. 4. Vocational guidance] I. Title.
TL152.B775   1985   629.28'7'023   85-11303
ISBN 0-516-01885-X

PICTURE DICTIONARY

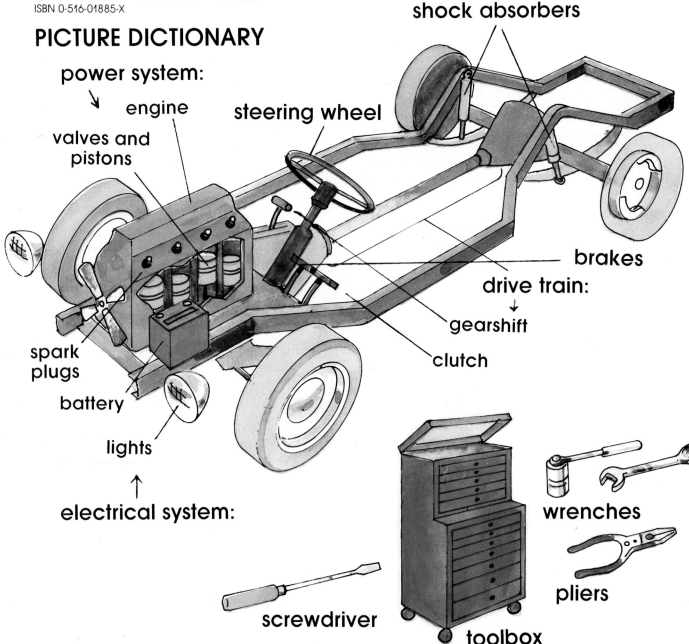

power system:
  engine
  valves and pistons
  spark plugs
  battery
  lights
electrical system:

shock absorbers
steering wheel
brakes
drive train:
  gearshift
  clutch

screwdriver
toolbox
wrenches
pliers

garage

gas station

auto showroom

repair shop

engine analyzer

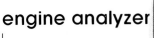

computer

high technology equipment

support system

parts dept.

grease and lube specialist

body shop

business office

high school/ trade school

electronics school

instructions

Auto mechanics work for gas stations (above) and for places that sell cars.

Where does a car owner take a car when it needs fixing or does not run?

Does the car go back to the place where it was bought?

Does it go to a garage or a gas station?

It goes to a shop that has good automobile mechanics.

auto showroom

garage

gas station

repair shop

Mechanics work hard.

Auto mechanics work
hard. They don't mind
getting their hands dirty.
That is part of the job.

If you can answer "yes" to the questions below, you may be on your way to becoming an auto mechanic.

computer

1. Do you like to work with cars?

2. Can you work a computer?

3. Can you read instructions?

4. Can you work math problems?

There was a time when an auto mechanic didn't need much training. But today's mechanic needs to know how cars work and also how to work computers.

New cars have computers in them. Mechanics need to understand what the

Computerized instrument panel found on a 1985 Corvette LCD

computers tell them. The
computers tell how a car
is operating and if
something is wrong with
the car.

instructions

toolbox

wrenches

pliers

screwdriver

Today's mechanic then must be able to fix what's wrong. Being able to read instructions and do math problems well are also very important.

An auto mechanic has a toolbox for regular tools, such as wrenches, pliers, and screwdrivers, and other special tools. The tools must be kept in order so they can be found quickly when needed.

Mechanics use special tools to repair engines.

A mechanic must have manual dexterity. Manual dexterity means the ability to use the hands quickly and well.

Woman mechanic tests an engine part.

A mechanic also
needs a good mind that
can solve problems. He
or she must track down
what might be wrong
and what might need
fixing.

Mechanic checks an engine.

When a mechanic takes an engine apart, all the parts must be kept in order. After the engine is fixed, the parts must be put back in the right order.

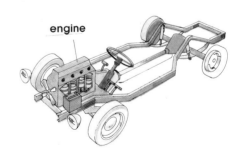
engine

Suppose you take out six pieces in order—1, 2, 3, 4, 5, and 6. You have to put them back together in backward order—6, 5, 4, 3, 2, 1. Then the engine will work!

Sometimes a mechanic may have to fix part of the car's electrical system. An electrical

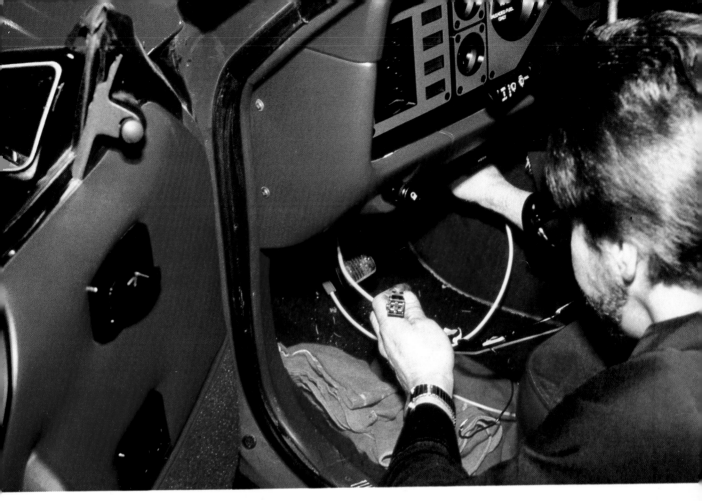

Mechanic replaces ignition wires.

system includes such things as the battery, the spark plugs, and the lights.

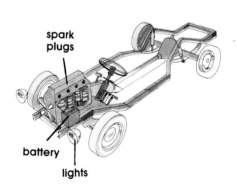

The mechanic plugs a small computer into the

car's engine to test the electrical system. The computer tells what might need to be fixed. Then the mechanic must know how to fix the problem.

An auto mechanic has to know about the car's power system. The power system is what helps keep a car going. Some of the parts of the power system are the valves

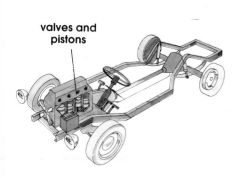

valves and pistons

Mechanics learn how to check and repair spark plugs. Spark plugs are part of the electrical system.

and the pistons. If they don't work properly, a computer will show the mechanic what needs to be fixed.

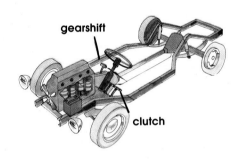

gearshift

clutch

Another car system is the drive train. It includes such things as the gear shift and the clutch. In cars with a clutch, the driver changes gears by hand. Many cars do not have a clutch. The gears change automatically.

Then there are the systems that have to do with steering, stopping, and the suspension of the car. The steering system includes the

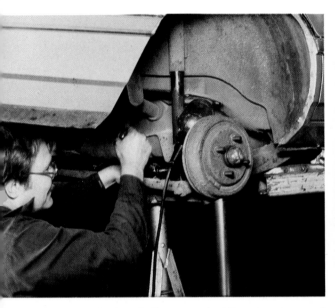

Brakes (left) are part of the stopping system. Shock absorbers (right) are part of the suspension system.

steering wheel. The stopping system involves the brakes. And the suspension system uses shock absorbers. The shock absorbers are springs that make for a smoother ride.

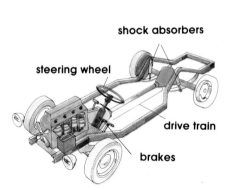

shock absorbers

steering wheel

drive train

brakes

Front-end technician works with a student.

An auto mechanic does not work alone. The people helping a mechanic are called a support system.

Large car repair shops have a parts department. The parts department manager uses a computer to keep track of what parts are in the shop. There are thousands of parts for the many models of cars made each year. These parts range from a small screw to a large tire.

parts dept.

A lube specialist changes oil in a customer's car.

grease and lube specialist

Some mechanics are grease and lube specialists. ("Lube" is short for "lubricating oil.") All cars need periodic checks to see that the parts are running smoothly. A grease and lube specialist sees that this task is done properly.

The body shop is where a car is repaired

body shop

if there is damage to the frame or outside. A body shop specialist must find the right color of paint, iron out a crumpled fender, and fix such things as a door that is out of line with its frame.

Getting a new car ready for its owner is another job. The car needs to be checked over, tested, and washed.

Finally, the business office of an automobile shop is a busy place. This is where the bills are made out and records are kept.

business office

Computers keep track of the many business

Mechanics must keep a record of the hours spent and the work done on each job.

operations. But the people who work in the office also need to know something about the automobile business.

People who want to become auto mechanics

Students learn how to fix a flat tire.

**high school/
trade school**

today may have a better
chance if they graduate
from a high school rather
than a trade school.

After graduation they
can attend special

schools. For example, at electronics schools a student learns how to read and understand computers that are used in automobiles.

electronics school

Companies that make cars also have special courses. They help a mechanic keep up with all the changes in new cars.

A mechanic must be aware of new developments.

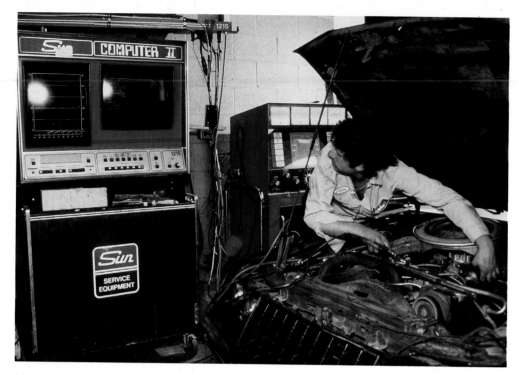

Mechanic uses a computerized engine analyzer.

Today's cars are products of high technology.

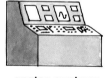

engine analyzer

Today's auto mechanics have to use high technology equipment, such as computerized engine analyzers. They must be able to fix the

Mechanics must know how an engine works in order to repair it properly.

problems that are found.
A mechanic needs a
good support system of
people to help keep
cars, buses, and trucks
working.

Would you like to be
an auto mechanic?

WORDS YOU SHOULD KNOW

brake (BRAYK)—a device for slowing down or stopping. Most cars today use a combination of disc and drum brakes.

computer (kum • PYOO • ter)—an electronic machine that may perform high-speed math problems. Or it may assemble, store, and then give back information that has been collected in a program.

drive train (DRYVE TRAYN)—a series of gears, shafts, clutches, and hydraulic devices. These parts work together to move a car forward or backward.

electrical system (ih • LEK • trih • kil SISS • tim)—the system in a car that consists of the starting system, the accessory system, the ignition system, and the charging system. It gets the car going and operating through the use of electricity.

high technology (HI tek • NAHL • uh • gee)—the body of knowledge that produces, through the use of electronics, the tools necessary to practice skills and extract information

manual dexterity (MAN • yoo • ul dex • TAIR • ih • tee)—the ability to work well with the hands

parts department (PARTS dih • PART • ment)—the storeroom where individual car parts, both small and large, are stored for use

piston (PIST • un)—a solid cylinder that fits snugly into a large cylinder and moves back and forth by pressure of gas or steam

power system (POW • er SISS • tim)—most cars are powered by either a diesel or a gasoline engine. Both are internal combustion engines. They operate on a heat expansion principle. When the engines are fired, the parts begin to operate. The oiling and cooling systems of a car function when the power system is in operation.

shock absorber (SHAHK ab • ZOR • ber)—a device in a car that cushions the impact of a bump

valve (VALV)—any device that regulates or controls the flow of a fluid

INDEX

auto showroom, 5
battery, 15
bills, 24
body shop specialist, 23
brakes, 19
business office, 24
clutch, 18
computers, 7, 8, 9, 15, 16,
     17, 21, 24, 27
drive train, 18
electrical system, 14, 15, 16
electronics schools, 27
engine, 13, 14, 16
engine analyzers, 28
frame, 23
garage, 5

gas station, 5
gears, 18
gear shift, 18
grease and lube specialists,
     22, 23
high school, 26
high technology, 28
instructions, 7, 10
lights, 15
lube specialists, 22, 23
manual dexterity, 11
math problems, 7, 10
new cars, 24
parts department, 21
pistons, 17
pliers, 10
power system, 16, 17

problems, solving, 12
reading, 7, 10
records, 24
schools, 26, 27
screwdrivers, 10
shock absorbers, 19
spark plugs, 15
steering system, 18
steering wheel, 19
stopping system, 18, 19
support system, 20, 29
suspension system, 18, 19
toolbox, 10
trade school, 26
valves, 16
wrenches, 10

PHOTO CREDITS

Hillstrom Stock Photo:
  © Don and Pat Valenti—4 (top), 11 (2 photos), 19 (2 photos), 25, 28
  © Norma Morrison—6
  © Warren Coleman—20

Journalism Services:
  © Hank DeGeorge—4 (bottom), 15
  © Joseph Jacobson—Cover

Campbell-Ewald Company—9

Nawrocki Stock Photo:
  © Jim Wright—12

Tom Stack and Associates:
  © Jim McNee—13

Image Finders:
  © Bob Skelly—17 (2 photos), 26, 29

Texaco Inc./American Petroleum Institute—22

Cover: Racing mechanic

ABOUT THE AUTHOR

Dr. Ray Broekel has written over 1,000 stories and articles for children. He has also written over 150 books on many topics for both children and adults. He has learned that an author needs to go to the right people to find out about a subject. Then he sits down and writes about them.

Dr. Broekel also teaches people how to write. And finally, he has perhaps one of the sweetest hobbies in the world. He is known as the number-one authority in the world on candy bar history.